INSTRUCTIONS

⊙ FOR ⊙

PATCHWORK

✳ PRICE, 15 CENTS. ✳

Copyrighted, 1884, by
J. F. INGALLS, Publisher.

Windham Press is committed to bringing the lost cultural heritage of ages past into the 21st century through high-quality reproductions of original, classic printed works at affordable prices.

This book has been carefully crafted to utilize the original images of antique books rather than error-prone OCR text. This also preserves the work of the original typesetters of these classics, unknown craftsmen who laid out the text, often by hand, of each and every page you will read. Their subtle art involving judgment and interaction with the text is in many ways superior and more human than the mechanical methods utilized today, and gave each book a unique, hand-crafted feel in its text that connected the reader organically to the art of bindery and book-making.

We think these benefits are worth the occasional imperfection resulting from the age of these books at the time of scanning, and their vintage feel provides a connection to the past that goes beyond the mere words of the text.

As bibliophiles, we are always seeking perfection in our work, so please notify us of any errors in this book by

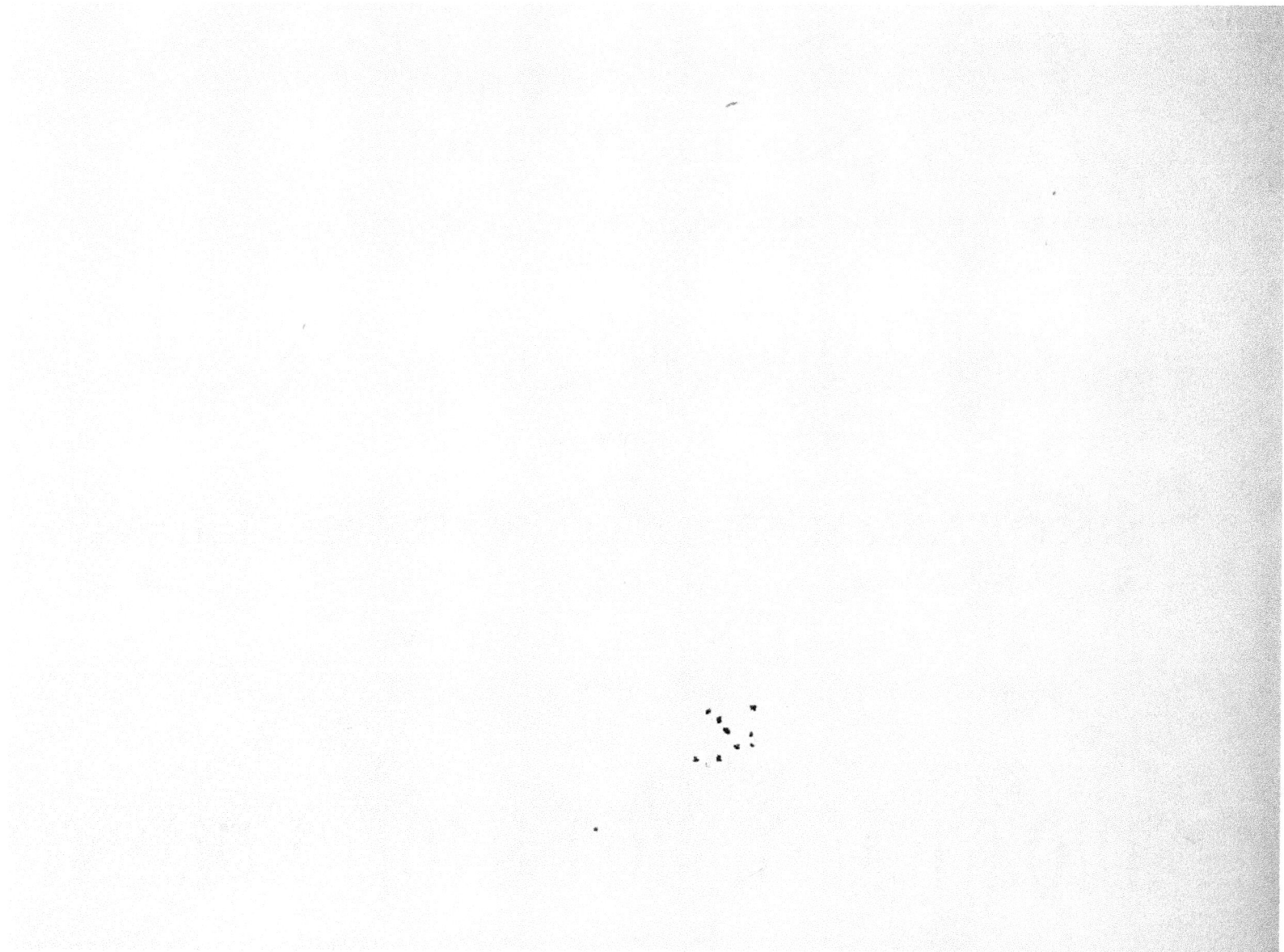

INSTRUCTIONS FOR PATCHWORK.

A NEW BOOK OF

PATTERNS AND INSTRUCTIONS

FOR MAKING

FANCY PATCHWORK.

PRICE, 15 CENTS.

Instructions for Patchwork.

It is very popular to make Tidies, Mats, Sofa Pillows, Afghans, Bed Spreads, etc., of small pieces of Silk and Satin.

Take a piece of some firm goods the size you want the article. Upon this baste the silk and satin pieces in all sorts of irregular shapes, turning in the raw edges. Then work the edges of each piece with different designs of the POINT RUSSE stitches. In working these stitches, use embroidery silk. That called "waste" embroidery silk, that comes (mixed colors) in short lengths, is the best and cheapest to use,

The Silk and Satin pieces are much prettier with snow flake stitches, sprays of flowers and outline designs of children's heads, bugs, etc., worked on them. Work the designs before joining to the other pieces.

We think the illustrations, in this book, of Crazy Patchwork, Point Russe and Snow Flake stitches will give you a better idea of the work than any explanations we can write.

POINT RUSSE STITCH FOR EDGES.

POINT RUSSE STITCHES.

POINT RUSSE STITCHES.

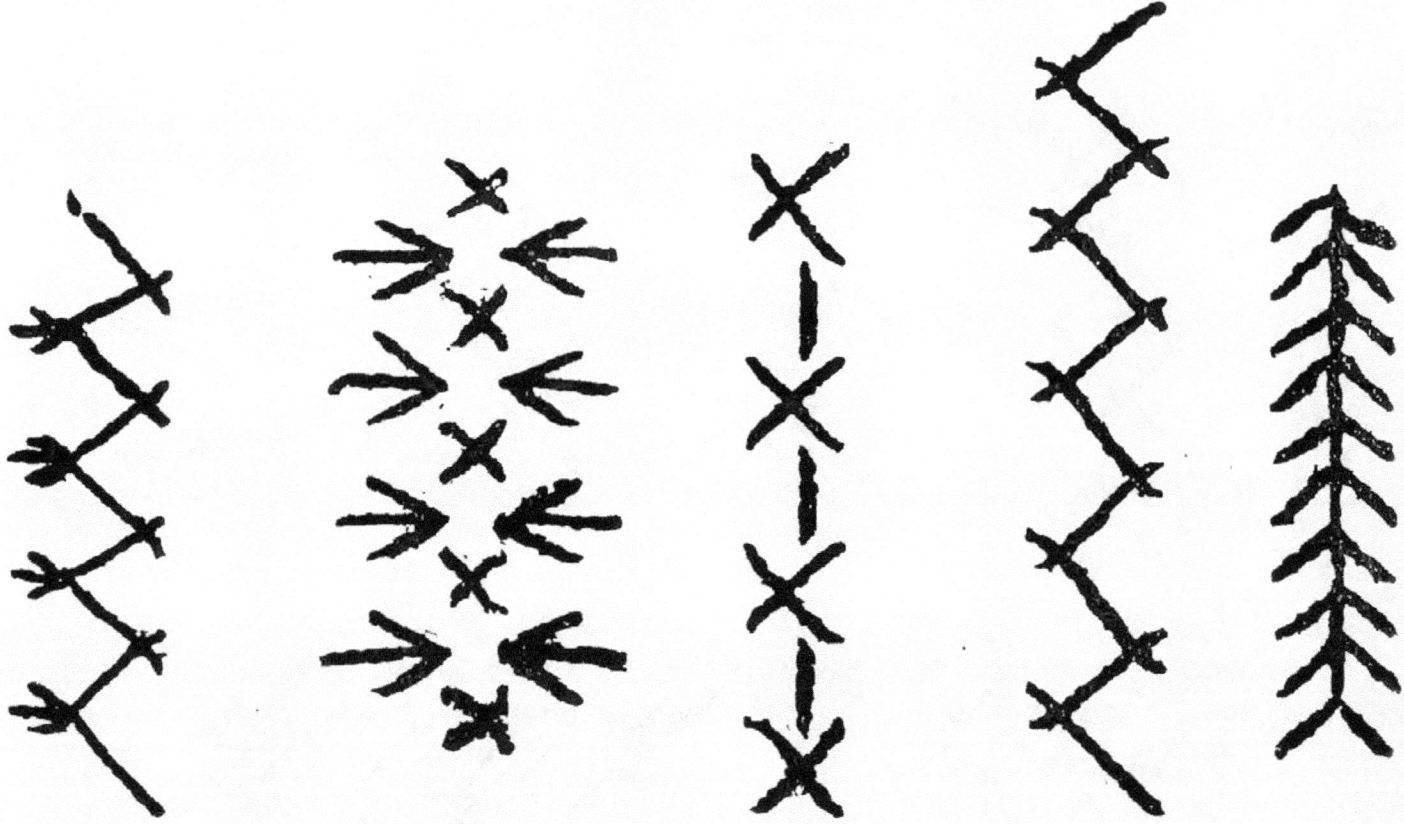

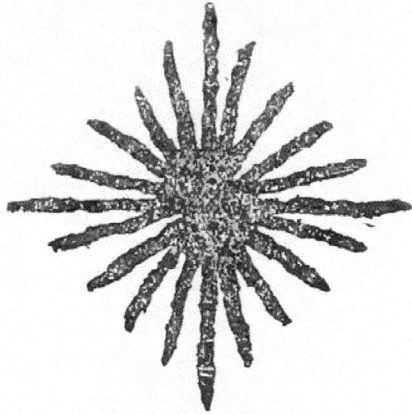

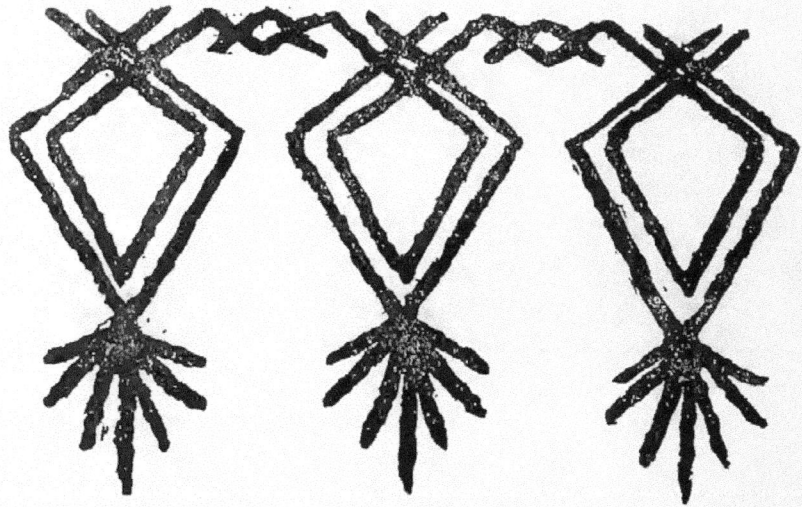

POINT RUSSE STITCHES.

POINT RUSSE STITCHES.

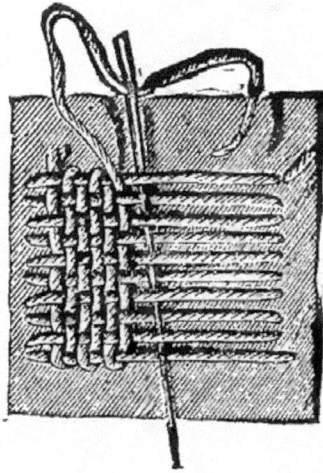

POINT RUSSE STITCHES.

POINT RUSSE STITCHES.

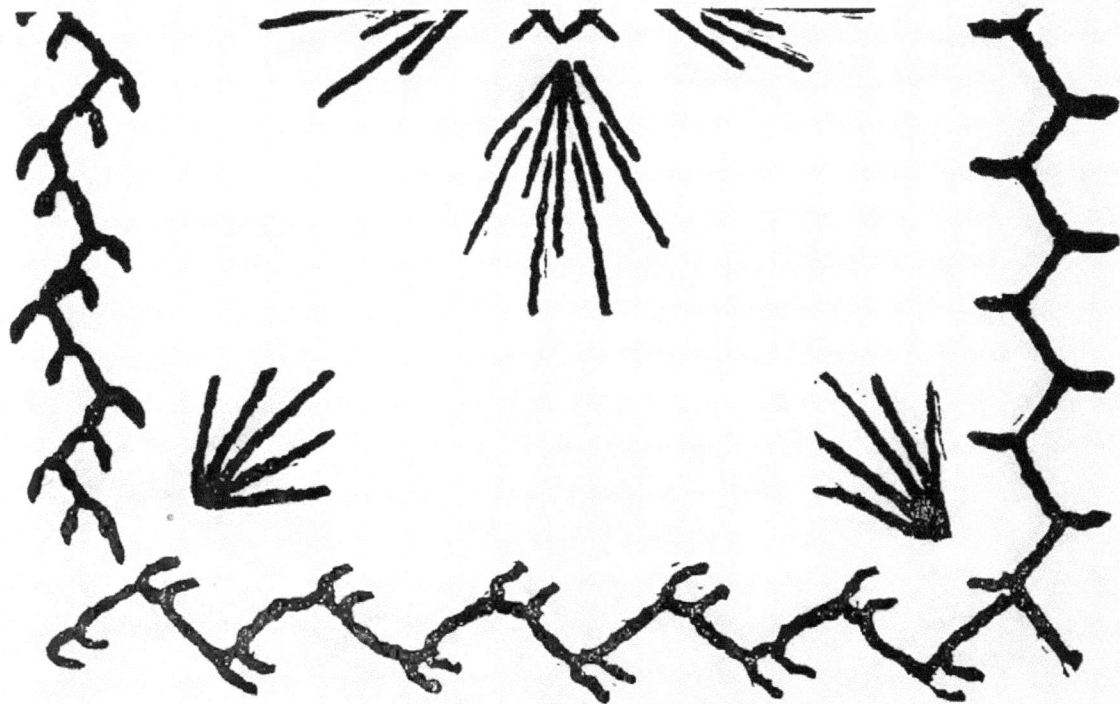

POINT RUSSE STITCHES.

POINT RUSSE STITCHES.

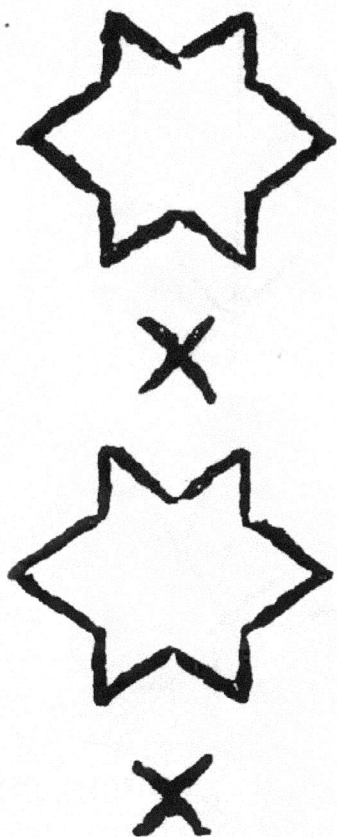

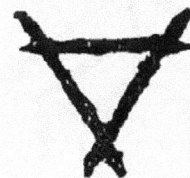

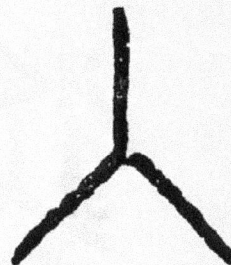

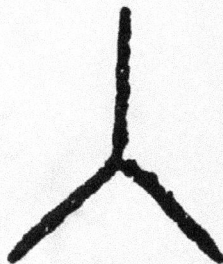

SNOW FLAKE STITCHES.

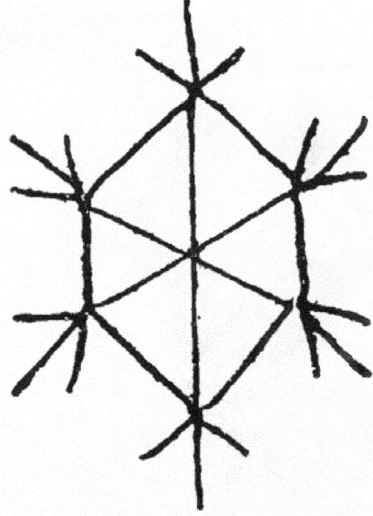

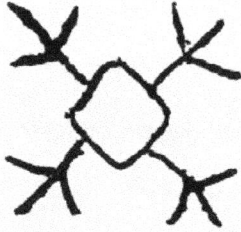

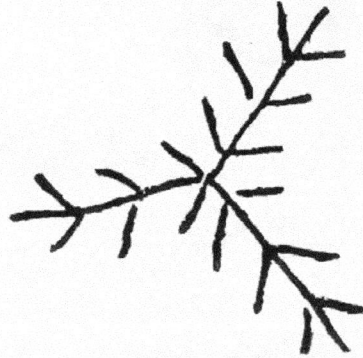

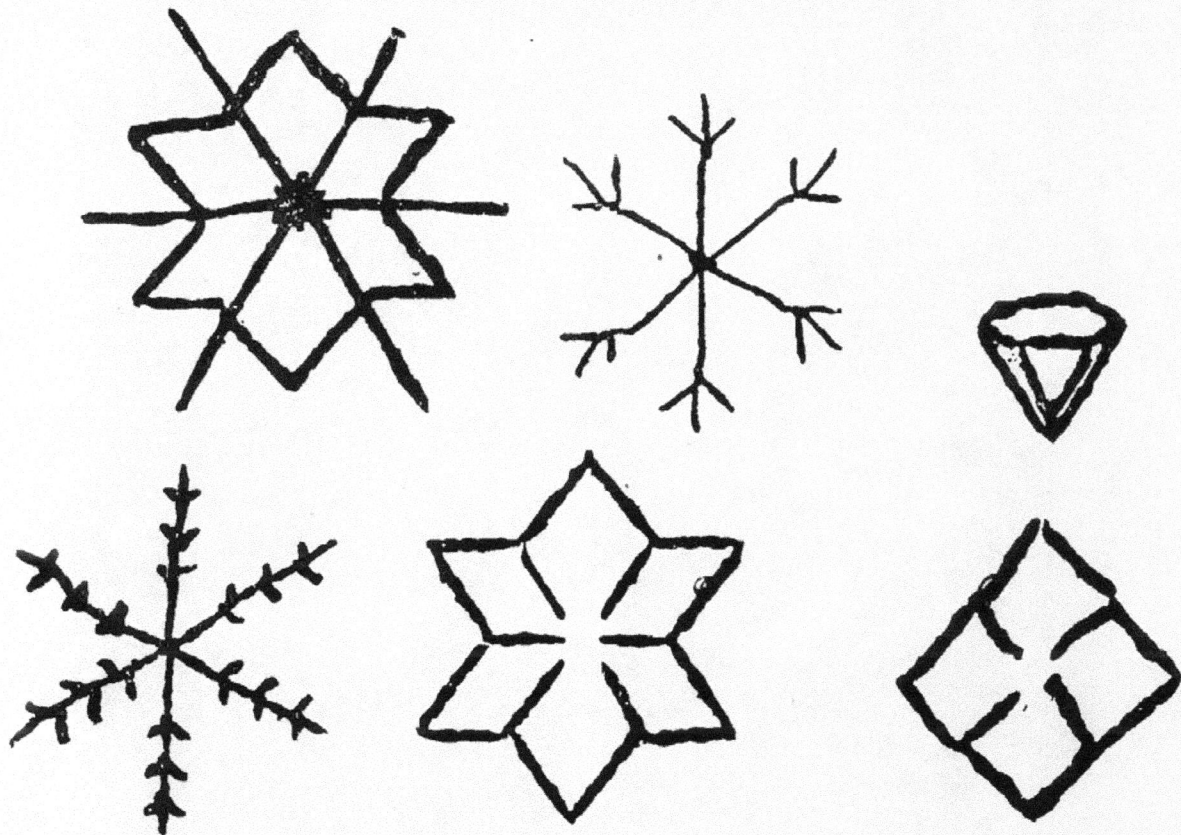

SNOW FLAKE STITCHES.

BLOCK OF CRAZY PATCHWORK.

BLOCK OF CRAZY-PATCHWORK.

THIS engraving shows how a block, formed of scraps of silk, satin, or velvet may be richly elaborated with embroidery combining a variety of the Point Russe stitches, illustrated in this book. The scraps are in all sorts of shapes, and are arranged in all sorts of conceivable ways.

EMBROIDERY OF DARNING STITCHES.

THIS design forms an effective decorative feature in the block of Crazy Patchwork. It is worked on a plain piece of silk or satin. It is first outlined, and then the spaces are embroidered with the stitches.

EMBROIDERY OF DARNING STITCHES.

TABLE SCARF.

A HANDSOME scarf, as appropriate for a mantel, piano, etc., as it is for a table, is here illustrated. It is made of felt cloth, edged at the ends with a fringe formed of heavy silk tassels alternating with large plush pendants. A little above the fringe is applied a broad band of Crazy Patchwork embroidery, formed of three blocks of Patchwork, separated by bands of velvet ribbon applied and decorated with a variety of fancy stitches done with mixed colors of embroidery silk. Bordering the band on each side is a row of wide velvet ribbon, blind-sewed on. The blocks of Patchwork may be very different in appearance. [See block of Crazy Patchwork.] The cloth may be of any color desired, and the velvet ribbon may be alike or contrast in color. Any kind of fringe preferred may be substituted for that illustrated.

TABLE SCARF,

BORDERS FOR CRAZY PATCHWORK.

A BROAD band of brocaded, plain or fancy velvet, silk, plush or satin, makes a handsome border. Black, dark garnet, deep crimson, navy-blue, ruby, violet, olive, purple, dark green, cardinal and brown are especially effective colors for borderings, the depth of their hues softening the brilliancy of the work, yet bringing out its beauty in the same way as a beautiful frame shows off a handsome painting.

QUILT OF SILK PATCHWORK.

THE quilt illustrated is made of light and dark blocks of silk cut and joined as illustrated. The blocks may be as large or as small as the maker likes or her material allows, and, of course, the size of the quilt is a matter of personal calculation, according to the dimensions of the bed it is to cover. The border consists of two shades of brocaded ribbon flatly joined, and the corners are squares of silk or satin, embroidered by hand in floral designs. The lining should also be of silk, but may be of fine muslin or Farmer's satin.

QUILT OF SILK PATCHWORK.

DECORATED BAND FOR FANCY WORK.

DECORATED BAND FOR FANCY WORK.

THIS band may be made of plaid silk or velvet ribbon, and is used to separate the strips of embroidery upon tidies, cushions, or any little fancy article requiring such an accessory to its component parts. The engraving shows how the stitches are made, and where they are located. The silk used for making them is of the gayest colors. This decorated band will also give you some ideas for working the edges of the Crazy Patchwork.

BLOCK PATCHWORK.

STAR PATCHWORK.

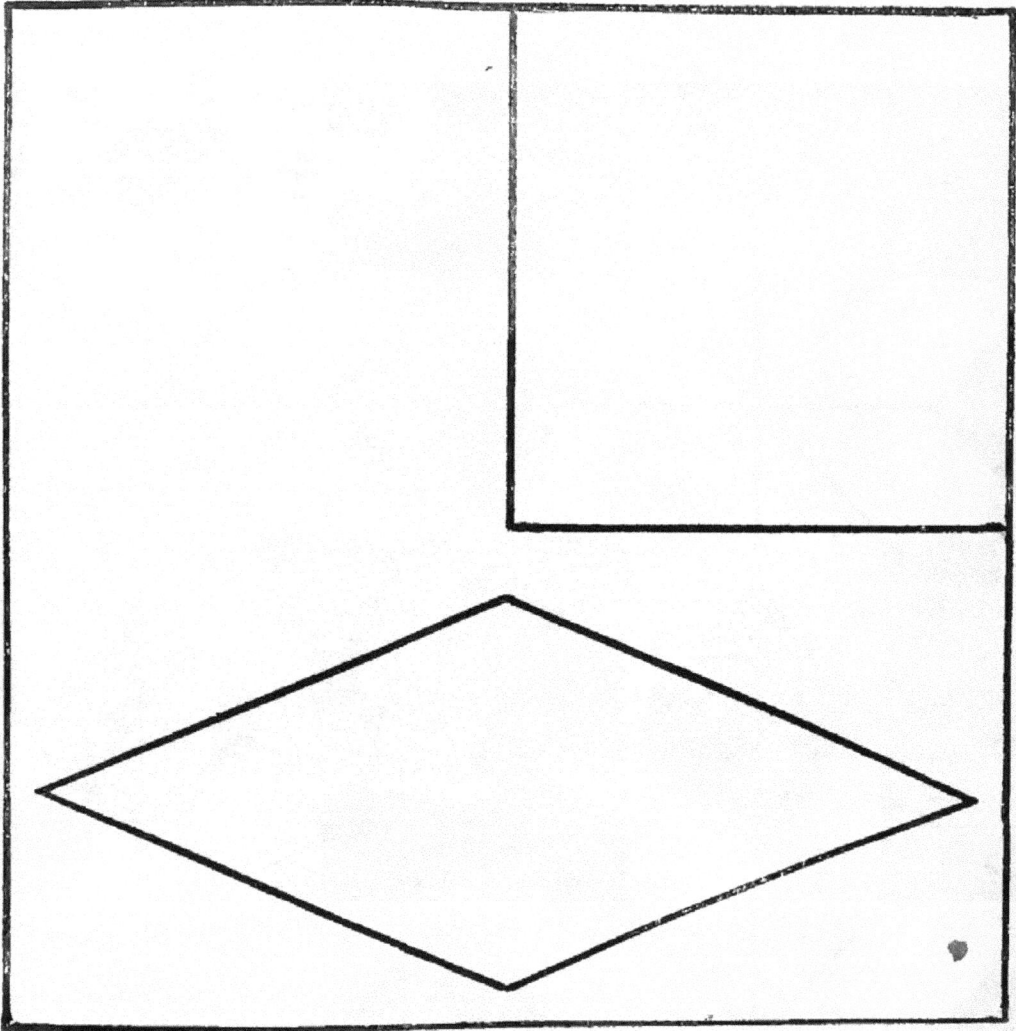

This page is left blank so that the patterns for the Star Patchwork can be cut out without spoiling the book, but if you have tracing paper it would be better to trace the lines. You can enlarge the patterns, or make them smaller, as you wish; but care must be taken that the right proportions are kept.

PATTERNS FOR BLOCK PATCHWORK.

www.ingramcontent.com/pod-product-compliance
Lightning Source LLC
Chambersburg PA
CBHW081233020426
42331CB00012B/3162